For Ian Chapman who began it all

Also compiled by Nanette Newman

GOD BLESS LOVE
LOTS OF LOVE
VOTE FOR LOVE
ALL OUR LOVE
THE FACTS OF LOVE

Cover by Sarah aged 5

First published 1985

© Bryan Forbes Ltd 1985

ISBN 0 00 195251 X

Made and printed in Great Britain by
William Collins Sons & Co Ltd Glasgow

# The Best of Love

A collection of children's sayings
compiled by

NANETTE NEWMAN

*love*
*Nanette*

COLLINS

# FOREWORD

When I finished <u>The Facts of Love</u>, the fifth
collection in the series that began with <u>God
Bless Love</u>, I fully expected it to be my last.
Yet the material still came pouring in from
schools, hospitals, parents, grandparents and
friends, and the temptation proved irresistible!

So I hope that this, another "final" book, will
give readers as much pleasure as it has given
me in putting it together.  While thanking the
many contributors I feel I must single out two
schools in particular - Meopham C.P. Infants
School, Meopham, Kent and Christchurch School,
Virginia Water.  But I owe a renewed debt to all
the young people whose words and drawings adorn
these pages, and to every one of them I say
Thank you very, very much.

Nanette Newman

NAN NET

BY TOBY

my rabbit was a ~~be~~ bachelor.

David aged 5

MY uncle has started to grow to Look Like a mouse.

Simon aged 5

Jesus had a cow and a donkey but I think he would rather have had a hamster.

Brent aged 6

It's sad for cows Because they're a swear word.

Sam aged 6

FRENDS

I call my friend Whity because
She is black and She calls me
blacky because I am white.
it makes us Laufe

Kate aged 8

My dad likes white people
black people chinese people but not
people from Tottenham.

Albie aged 7

I don't know when you get old but I
expect it's when you cant run any more

Rosalind aged 5

My granny doesn't wear tights
because once she fell over. Elizabeth aged 5

My next-door neighbour has
a stool her feet sit on. Mary aged 5

old people read to you

until they fall asleep

Craig aged 6

When old people go on holiday they
sit on deckchairs and wish they hadnt come

Amy aged 8

f you get old to qweekley you never groo up.

Winston aged 5

They put their helmit on a
chair when they go to bed.
Nicholas aged

If they stand in front
of your car you have to
stop.

David aged 6

He leaned right in the car
and my dad said he was drunk.

Scott aged 6

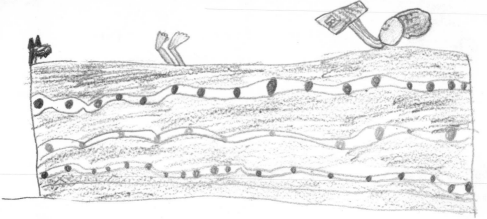

The queen Stays in the bath and does
a crossword puzzle on her day off    Richard aged

Our Queen does the
house work On her day
off.          Josh aged 7

Mrs Thatcher should do something
but Ive forgotten what it is

John aged 7

Mrs Thatcher was playing
Snakes and Ladders with the queen

Joanna aged 7

her day off Mrs Thatcher watches herself on
le.      Anne Marie aged 7

Auntie Iris came æ a the way from Skegness.

Steven aged 6

My sister says she eats men alive but shes only pretending.

Mandy aged 6

my dad has found a better mummy for us than the last one.

Michael aged 6

My Uncle is a riligous Maniac but I think he has another job as well.

Stephen aged 6

It's no good taking your dog to a
wedding because they don't like
Singing.

Martha aged 6

My brother didn't want to get Married He
wanted to take Me to Football

Caroline aged

My sister got her wedding dress off
Hilary's Mum because Hilary's Mum
didn't get married after all

Jenny aged 6

traffic wardens have to be cross
all day ells they lose there jobb. Tim aged

My dad says you must never hate anyone except traffic wardens.

Andrew aged 8

If a traffic warden sees you kissing in a car you get cramped

Alice aged 6

My best enemy is Mark.

David aged 6

A baby duzent know how to be norty.
It has to be tort.

Rosalie aged 7

If you do something very bad you can sell

your story to a newspaper.

Jake aged 9

People shouldnt kill babies when they are

just seeds.

Stephanie aged 6

When I put my new
coat on my hands were
hiding

Diana aged 5

I want to dance but
my feet won't let me.

My friend says Kissing is worse than haveing flu.

Caroline aged 6

A man fell in love with my auntie on a train but she pulled the cord and he stoped.

Liz aged 6

My mummy cried on my first day at school so I had to take her home.

Penny aged 5

If you're a nurse you have to be dessicated.

Sophie aged 6

we go to a hotel in France becausen we all get a penshun.

Toby aged 7

some words you are only allowed to say on television not in front of people.

Jonathan aged 6

I've collected money to save the Prince of whales.

Janet aged 6

If you're a princess you have to smile
even if you feel sick

Jason aged 7

When people start wars they never know how to stop. Alanda aged 6

I think war is exciting on television for real I think it is horrible

John aged 7

Help me Mummy

HELP

Army Army
Army Army

a deck chair got her

Sarah aged 5

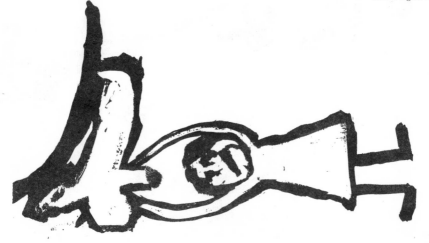

My brother cant work because hes 2 old. Hes 21.

Camela aged 8

People over here starve themselves to win prises but in Africa it kills you.

Kalima aged 9

They give you a lovely party when

you die.

Jamie aged 6

People keep their eyes open when they pray in case Jesus arrives

Adam aged 7

God is
wonderful
he.maked
the
holiworld
And
he
Maked
US all

Huw aged 6

ur vicar tells people off on Sundays but

es nice when he is out shopping.

Marsha aged 6

hey want money to stop the church

alling down but th vicar spends it aiwll on wine

Anthony aged 7

God Smoked a pipe not cigarettes.

Paul aged 5

Good by
For good

Peter aged 6